song unsung

54 POEMS

CHINA CANCIO

song unsung

~

"The feeling only I know is seeping through
As I walk on this journey alone
I wish you were with me."

~

Song Unsung is a collection of poetry about life, love and heartbreak, dark and raw emotions. This book is divided into three parts, and each part serves a different purpose.

Contents

PART THREE
DARK AND RAW

PART ONE

Life

There's always a time when

words are silent as nothing.

Even in nothing, you hear a hiss.

Nights scream louder;

Zephyr howls like the wolf.

When minds and dreams are tangled,

thrown into oblivion...

Is it better for humans to live forever?

Is it better for humans to disappear?

Is it better for us,

humans!

to join the winds;

the seas;

the lands.

Wouldn't it be nice for everything to be as one?

Blessed is the seagull

floating in bliss above the seas,

wings spread,

as if all which is below is under its dominion

There's always a time when

words are better be silenced.

Let God's breath—

the only song heard by his creation.

talking to the blue skies passing by

I don't hear them answer; their faces smile

the earth sings the songs of birds, of farmers, of life

I was young, yet to grow

I understand now; I didn't then

how grey adulthood can be

childhood, friendship, laughter

I do not wish to part from them

Can maturity contain purity?

miracles and dreams of the young ones

we built them while looking up at the sky—

blue skies that were reachable by our little hands

· · ·

feeling the pain of slowly losing my wings

knowledge reveals the magic of twilight

blue skies fade into my busy life

I wish to take back my ignorance

heart as green as grass

spirit as blue as the skies.

To the invisible tomorrow!

Our young hearts will move forward

With big smiles and high-pitched laughter

The occasional rain wipes our gloomy faces

You see, the earth is glowing.

Dreams are child's wings, we are not without it

To you, never-present tomorrow!

Our young hearts will move forward

Until our head is old, and wings are lazy.

Fly, little bird, fly

The world is too big but fly

The height is too high but fly

Your wings are small and weak; with all your might, fly!

These huge branches are strong and secure

Whispers of green leaves, a perfect tune for your song

How warm this nest is—so comfortable

But don't lie down forever to die.

Fly, little bird, fly

You'll be big someday... fly!

Spread those little wings and fly

Face the sun, sing your song, float in complete freedom.

. . .

Fly, little bird, fly

Bask in the abundance of creation

Soar high to the limitless horizon

Yes, little bird… fly and see how far you've come.

Let's go back home...

even if the journey seems endless

our feet and hearts, weary.

Surely, the loud roar of thunder will stop

the rain will calm down

and rainbow shall display God's gift.

Very soon, we will hear the songs of birds

the hymn of trees and wind

our mothers' bosom so warm and safe.

Let's go back home, shall we?

Let us be young again

taste the kiss of innocence

embrace the familiar scent

breath of home, heart's home.

Your scent is like an old book

Take me to your fantasy world

Light that sweeps away the dark clouds

A confirmation that clears confusion.

Your spirit shall abide in me

Cold air that gives peace at night

Steering wheel that drives through bends

You're the tranquil song played by the rain.

The palace where king and queen sleep;

Wisdom that guides many lives

Earthquake that shakes my weakness

And strength that builds my dream.

I am a wildflower

I am which makes nature scenic

taking roots in no specific places

God whispers I am untainted

growing freely, uncultivated

my tears taste sweet

ants gather to take a sip

but one slip of judgement

a regrettable torment

I may be ugly

I may be pretty

likable or despicable

I am necessary.

two energies—woven

sturdy, fragile, never permanent

remnants scatter, settle

new connections start to tangle

life, love—

the cycle never breaks

or will it?

a mother

a hymn

a baby

two souls but one

a tiny shack

the ocean

so humble

so proud

The hallway is now empty

So as my reflection in the mirror

I turn my gaze to the living room

To the rock garden

This entire house

Once filled with ruckus

Now, a screaming silence

Echoing in my ears

Reaching my aging soul.

stepping into emotions

from the stone-cold prison—

their faces, now vivid

the knot, now untied

and the fog has cleared

someone's calling; I pretend to not hear
no senses, no strength to struggle

back flat in bed, eyes to the ceiling
If I continue to lie down like this, would I fade away?

I raise my hand, looking at my ugly fingers
Is someone out there doing the same thing?

raise my heart to the sky
in simple things, I am able to fly

old songs endure, guiding my spirit
returning to the past, where I must belong

.   .   .

Why did my soul choose this body?

Would I be an angel if mama had not born me?

I long to take those steps

I have but one pair of footprints

only when I take those steps

I can leave an imprint on the road

those hidden footprints

connect and merge with others

only then I can finally say

on my deathbed

I was never alone.

I'm walking on wet ground
bare feet touch the grass
I see life in their green limbs
that's when I know the earth is happy.

The unseen passes through me
along with it, memories and wishes
I find myself reminiscing
that's when I realized creation is blessed.

I live in a world of fire, it is life and death
it is light, construction and destruction
that's when I understand choice.

I spread my arms to welcome existence.

This bliss I can't contain, I'm ablaze

eyes closed, I see infinity

that's when I'm convinced I exist.

I see but cannot reach
dandelions fly to the north
floating image on the field
a fantasy yet to be confirmed

fireflies open a dream
light uncovers reality
bare feet run to the grave
death opens heaven's gates

scent of old books a mystery
secret port of the dreamers
revelation reveals a puzzle
not playing defeats the scheme

This song is solace -
the song of an old man
Let me rest
I've been traveling alone
for a long time.
My feet, worn out
My heart has aged
My mind is satisfied
My journey is the color of sunset.
This weak vessel still carries a young soul -
soul inhales knowledge, exhales wisdom
so spring can breathe in... grow! endure!
When your head turns white as the mountain...
sing the old man's song.

What my heart has sought the most—
scent of the ground after the gentle rain,
breeze that carries the dew from wild grass,
ruffling seas in the foggy morning,
long love letter from the past,
smell of childhood through moist skin.

It's sad when you don't know your true value;
thus, you let people define you.
But how can you know your worth
when all your life you are led to believe,
and no one removes the blindfold.

PART TWO

Love and Heartbreak

I am back from a thorny path
rain's gloom welcomes my return
mud on my boots soiling my heart
gust of wind drying my soul.
spectacles and its broken glasses
I see clearly without them now
I see I am almost home, but
the flaming arrow catches up.
long shiny blade blinds my hope
suffocated heart desiring to beat
maneuvers and fear melting justice
a desired last wish, a denied last wish.

In the dark sky, a full moon

In the stream, a reflection

Ornamented path—blue and white flowers

Blooming more in the gloomy hours

Plain is the night

A garden in the moonlight

Scent of roses fills the air

Sobs—the only sound heard

A plain face gazing to the west

Ruminating about the past

Her sight to the serpentine course of the creek

The scenery, a melancholic masterpiece

linger

The blue hue surrounding dawn;

the smell of the sea reminds me of the past,

when innocence was evident in the laughter.

My heart is covered with morning mist;

Damp as the sand on my feet,

I can't seem to let go.

Fighting to forget, fighting to remember.

Looking up to the sky, not finding the answer.

Wasn't that life a treasure?

Rushing through the day for comfort;

When the night approaches,

I find myself living in the memories of you.

· · ·

The path that we both walked on

Far ahead, I couldn't find you.

All that's left is the echo of your song.

The clarity of reality; we are no longer who we were then.

The wind has blown, separated our paths.

Yet the shadow of the past hangs on.

You're here again—
every drop is accompanied with pain
cool ambiance brings disgust to my soul
Stop! Please don't fall.

Hate to reminisce that sweet past
joy gives heavy feeling
memories—I hate so much
I'd rather live in solitude.

Stop! Please stop falling!
Torture is the best you bring
along with the clouds you gather
is the image of the man, my dearest.

Missing someone you must not see,

let alone touch, is like

stabbing your own chest, and

you still keep doing it knowing

it will lead to your own destruction;

Missing someone from afar,

someone who is oblivious of you, is

living in a world so grey

hopeless, lifeless, and yet

never painless.

ocean breeze

carries the chill of midnight;

steadily cooling down my fury.

maple leaf

disturbs the still puddle;

displeasingly muddling my reflection.

time

persistently clings in my skin and soul;

and its unapologetic way of proving I reap what I sow.

Your voice, as soft as whisper,

pierces the deepest part of my being;

continuously revealing my truest form.

When the plumeria tree scatters its blossoms

The sunset hue engulfs the gazebo

With cool breeze almost freezing the teacup

A moth comes in avoiding the flowers.

Time has covered the world with dried petals

But the plumeria tree remains standing

Occasionally accompanied by a moth

Habitually avoiding its scattered blossoms.

Paths and parallel worlds
meet me there...
Unchained hearts are bound,
broken puzzles,
love falls as cherry blossoms.
There's blue sky behind those clouds,
joy, sorrow... the hearts that yearn
hidden from the unseeing eyes.
How many of me cherishes that road?
I'll meet you on the same path
in a thousand parallel worlds.
The bench under the tree,
the boulder by the road...
long forgotten memories
swing back as déjà vu.

How many times have we met?

Dreams may be open doors.

I shall see you in the past, in the future

our numerous lives may have already crossed

the galaxy a million times.

Until we recognize and ask

along those paths and parallel worlds,

the unseeing eyes will continue to walk

on unknown roads.

Rain—falling heavily from the dark clouds
Falling painfully down her dead-pale skin.

Rain—you are blowing wind, so cold
Making her shiver under that black coat.

Rain—bringing cover to joker's gloom
Giving the old hermit a companion.

Will you ever stop falling on that lone road?
A silhouette is crumpled nearby, injured.

secret romance at sunset

Your voice

carries me like the wind

through the fields

before the sunset.

When the cricket can finally

call for his mate

after the long wait

I get to hear your tale

behind this solitary tree.

Alas, this heart will soon

sing of longing

when the sun rises

the gods cast their spells

in the skies again.

When the waters

mirror the hues of twilight

treading the usual track

hem of my dress, soiled

strands of hair

dancing in autumn breeze

giving away

my secret anticipation.

Midnight...

Silence...

Moonlight...

Shadow...

Blade...

Blood...

Darkness...

Silence...

Will there be a right time?
Should I wait for the petals to fall?
Maybe when the pain goes numb?

I can't take the step
Your eyes reflect someone else's
I don't cause your smiles

Despair burns at my throat
Looking down, tears fall
But even those get lost in the rain

The feeling only I know is seeping through
As I walk on this journey alone
I wish you were with me.

The earth is bleeding.
Wondering when the service
Would come to an end.

The sun is not smiling.
Agonizing for being alone
In the sky's joyous lights.

The sea is roaring with grief.
Breaking the peace
By crashing the rocks.

Music is not gentle.
Cutting the time of the present
To the past's precious moments.

. . .

Loving someone

who doesn't know you exist

is suicide and nobody finds your body.

Why is the moon melancholic?

in the vastness of the sky

I see the trail of her woes

every drop, a throb

and my heart is a bucket

entranced by her desolate state

in her melancholy, the moon never fails

unescorted yet appeasing

heartbeats playing the tune

seemingly enjoying the torment

she must have always known

she is the only moon

and the earth is fine with it.

I hope the sun comes out and shoves the gloom of today

So I could catch sight of the rays hitting the windowpane

Or get a glimpse of your shadow across the fence

As you hurry along to catch a glimpse of your sunshine.

You pass by me
like a gentle breeze before a storm
Skipping through the leaves
like glimmers of light before sunset

Shoving the fields aside
running after you
leaves falling
wind calling

My eyes caught
that faint smile, orange skies
I'll wait for the day when we see
ourselves in each other's eyes

.   .   .

From dawn till night

till summer flies

I'll hold on tight

Dream to dream dies

Till the showering light

opens our hearts once again

Words unnecessary

smile for we both understand

Colors flood the sky...

fireworks!

like dancing flame in the hearts

of those in love,

beauty cracks into sparks—

Love.

Watching the gloomy night blissfully lit,

she waits and waits and waits.

Blood-red rose in the vase,

she's a scenery in the balcony.

I wish he could see her sun-colored hair flowing

as gentle breeze shower in its glory.

Beyond the castles, beyond the loud cheers and celebration,

who would hear her silent howl?

...like a lone wolf

calling for a comrade under the proud moon.

...like a wildflower by the cliff

that no man picks.

When iris overpowers the rose,

she witnesses them taste the nectar of first kiss.

Does love outshine diamonds?

...priceless! is it really?

Love defeats life;

Love, too, is darker than night

...weapon or shield, poison or antidote.

While she drinks the venom it offers,

while she bleeds by crushing the thorns,

walking above the raging waves,

heart's trickery—

malice mocks so she can see no more

and distinction between sanity and lunacy is faint,

...requited or not, good or evil

Love plays the role, masterfully.

PART THREE

Dark and Raw

confessions of a loser

Is it too late for me? Is it?
Am I left behind for good?
Am I a casualty of this unending battle?
Am I?

Glitters of hope shower upon them
Brand-new voices tickle the classic hearts
Hymns and rhythms reverberate like breeze and thunder
Stages and arenas vibrate and tremble.

I'm drowning in the deafening applause
Surrounded by everything that's huge.
Below the blinding light, it's dim
I am here but where?

.   .   .

I remove myself, uprooted, withdrawn

Somewhere, to an invisible fortress

Sob, smile, laugh

Alone in this Comfort Zone.

Everything is completely dark now

Still, I hear brand-new voices tickle the classic hearts

I squeak, no one answers... do they even want to listen?

I drown in the deafening applause; muted... erased.

if you don't feel like yourself

you don't recognize who you are

there is something wrong

you must have done something in pretense

trying to be someone else

you must be guilty

denying yourself of your true self

your core is telling you to stop

be wary of the tiny voice in your heart

it is pleading

you are not a counterfeit

Dear friend, Philip

Aren't you tired?

Aren't you suffering enough?

I see your tears have turned red

Your limbs shattered.

I remember the day of your birth

Foreign lands rejoiced

You were a blessing

Caged in return.

You were once a boy

Silently crying in the midst of confusion

Like a sweet orphan whom adults fight to adopt

Only to be made a slave.

. . .

My dear friend, Philip

You struggled and wailed

You were released

Free to dance, and free to fly.

Have you danced enough?

Have your little, fragile wings grown enough?

Once again, you are captured, chained and mocked!

Dear friend, Philip

Is the blood running through your veins still that of Philip?

Your mind has been corrupted; can no longer recognize yourself.

Your voice is frail; your torch is almost out.

My dear friend, Philip

Is freedom the fight of the weak, or the strong?

Does freedom mean submission or resistance?

Is freedom death of identity?

Does freedom give you freedom?

A silent night, a silent heart
Only stars are loud tonight
This summer will be a cold one
I wonder.

Steam is floating
Soon, you'll see it no more
As it joins the dust and wind
I'll have this cold coffee then.

Warm smiles, cold hearts
How have we become hypocrites
When time comes we admit it
Boulders freeze in winter.

faceless

I'm thrown into the void where faceless monsters reside.

I can't trust anyone but myself.

They speak of their identities so loud, so proud;

I am almost deceived.

With all my might, I run towards nothingness;

The black spell of these faceless follows me.

In the dark, glitters of counterfeit stones whisper and sing;

I am mesmerized.

I'm awakened by a weak cry—

I mustn't allow them to borrow my face!

For when I do, I'll never get it back,

and I will be faceless as they are.

What can I do when all I see is shadows?

Their black hands are creeping, feeling my skin.

What must I do when smoke is filling up the hole in me?

And I suffocate...

Frozen, I hear my mind laughing. Who am I mocking?

Void is bottomless, vanity is infinite.

What I'm attracting, I'm attracted to.

I watch myself turn into that monster

wearing countless faces—and so, I am Faceless.

Fingers are the judge

Words are the verdict

Thoughts—prison.

She can't control the words they spit

can't control their emotions.

Even though she can't embrace it...

Accept it. Stay silent.

Let them cuss and agonize, that's their choice

Yes, stones do hurt but be patient

Soon, their mouth will grow weary.

Isn't it better to stop it that way

Than to make this war endless?

Putting a single grain of salt into a glass of pure water

As lies and accusations made true by a tiny, misconstrued evidence.

Sometimes, denying is admitting.

It's necessary to just stay silent this time.

Courage is a must but know when to

back down for the greater good.

Rumors—prison of the accused.

Devoured by its mouth, she is gagged, consumed

Solidarity becomes a blessing and a curse

When day is night, darkness engulfs inside out

Of all there is on earth, it is the most deadly -

...spoils, breaks, kills.

Innocent or calloused hearts and guilty ones

All but the same in the eyes of the biased judge.

I always find myself falling towards infinity

I can't pick myself up

Lies pile up like a tower of stories

Which ones are made-up? Which ones are real?

When did I start putting on this mask? Who helped me put it on?

In this masquerade party, who must I point my fingers to?

Pretending... like this cold coffee on a rainy day

I am building something I can't recognize

All my fears are echoed in the rain, lightning brings with it a shadow

I run but not moving; it's still there, watching me

I hear the thunder mocking... I'm exposed!

Lies become truths; as honey into the ocean

Garbage makes pits; I jumped into the quicksand.

Move your bony little finger, let out a sign of soul

Just a bit of strength, just a little more

Stay with mama; whose eyes never dry, only her throat

Move your bony little finger, let out a sign of soul.

What a sight! Whose skin is it so new, so wrinkled?

Will the sun shine its light to the gloomy ones?

But the sun is mocking them; each ray a lash so deadly

Night's darkness, a gift; moon's humble beams, hope.

So move your bony little finger, let out a sign of soul

You, tiny one! Mama's gold and diamonds—Oh, tiny soul!

Become mama's night, moon, vessel of courage, river of life

Grab mama's finger, entwine... "My child, my soul."

Money can't make someone happy

But it sure can make life miserable.

Like a writer without ink

A poet who can't write poems

A knight without his sword

A tone-deaf singer in the middle of the night.

Money can't make someone happy

But it sure can make life miserable.

Saving for the future that has already come

When flesh becomes food

When the mighty fertilizes the soil

And bones - the only evidence of existence.

Money chuckles... mocking!

As lunatics laugh at their lunacy.

barely eight

father—a deep machete cut on one leg

mother—wounds all over the body

life forces its ways

life is a brawl

we fly to a land unknown

we are a spectacle

idle talks and hush hush!

don't let the subject hear yah!

the ruffles calm down

wounds healing

town is at peace again

. . .

I see newcomers

idle talks and hush hush!

and we join in…

don't let the subject hear yah!

Here she is again, singing that song

Does anyone hear her lamentations?

Be kind enough and stop for a moment

And listen...

Yes, the song that no one understands

People are cursing; afraid at the same time

She doesn't mind; her voice joins the rain and thunder

While humans pull their blankets, ignoring her cry.

I'm running

Bare feet

No footsteps

I'm thirsty

Dry throat

No water

I'm dizzy

No sleep

No bed

I trip

Stand up

Run again

I'm shouting

Help me!

They're running

I'm crying

No tears

It's painful

I'm grabbing

My dream

Got it!

Another one

Grab it

Got it!

They grab

Some miss

Some reach

Still wanting

Still grabbing

Getting, Failing

Chasing life

Chasing winds

Still wanting...

I am drowning
All I see is darkness
I try to grasp
The ocean swallows me.

The storm is never ceasing
Lightning illuminates vastness
My hope melts to nothing
Captured by my own escape.

I kick the water hard
I'm pinned
I mourn in silence
My world is wilting away.

. . .

My body is heavy

My soul is light

I give up the struggle

Let the waters carry me.

I remember the barren field—

glitter of life I see no more
the invisible stalking
day and night
hunger glooms the land.

my throat is dry, lips cracked
I trek from deserted town to towns
I seek refuge in the ruins of fallen kingdoms
I am the king of a multitude of stones and pebbles.

attending banquets of empty tables
Behold! My belly is bloated. Am I full?
Like a drunken man staggering, stumbling, crawling

hunger corrupts me of intelligence and consciousness.

Wind will soon reap my life.

Earth will eat my flesh.

My skeleton shall live forever

famished.

the unending

Thrust into the world of madness;

a puzzle forever be unsolved.

Joy, sadness, merciful peace of death;

moments undetermined... is it real or a dream?

Chasing the uncertainty of the wind;

mocked by the certainty of uselessness.

Perplexing that one knows he's dying;

scent of death—the unending mystery.

I enjoy being alone
away from other humans
half-hardheartedly I laugh
I cringe at my façade

maybe I miss the buzzing
the alarming horns of cars
tired and angry strangers
faces I forget in seconds

the visible particles of dust
crawling on my sticky skin
the dizzying smell of smoke
fills my lungs and brain

. . .

maybe I miss the feeling

the pain and inconveniences

or maybe I want to justify

I am fine the way I live.

Those were the dark days of humanity…

When mothers devoured their babies

When children fed on raw flesh and blood

When human skeletons were planted as trees

Those were the dark days of humanity…

When stones were the verdict to the weak

When sky was red; when clouds were smoke

When ground was vultures' table

Those were the dark days of humanity…

When a drop of humor was nonexistent

When tears quenched the thirst

When laughter was feasting wolves

Those were the dark days of humanity.

· · ·

When death had no beginning and end

When wails outlived the future

When hearts were grim, nurtured in sewage

The dark days of humanity... has it ended yet?

Swayed like branches during a storm
My faith is not strong enough to stand firm
Consequently, I walk on this narrow path
Towards the precipice where vanity lies.

Clearly, I see the abyss from where I stand
I can either stop or continue to jump
As vain as kings and queens in their kingdoms
I crown myself with vomit and venom.

I drink and get drunk from all of my worldly possessions
But I get thirsty and thirstier the more I hoard
I say I live to please and deplete my life
Evidently now, I am exhausted and tired.

. . .

I try and try harder to cleanse my soul

Swayed like branches during a storm

I find myself crowned with more vomit and venom

I fall towards oblivion; heavy and worn.

she doesn't know where it ends
the bend in the road keeps going
I have known her for a long time
but I still don't know what she wants.

It's my fate! I say
when hope is clearly amiss
she cried herself out
not knowing why she does
there's something missing inside
or is it empty from the start?

Where do we go from here?
like storms that ultimately stops
like the ball against the wall

like bubbles in the shore

Where do we go from here?
Where does she go from here?
she doesn't know where it ends
the bend in the road keeps going...

she tends to get so worked up
she spits venomous knives
He says,
"Get over here, I've been waiting for you for quite a while."

Thank you!

Thank you for purchasing and reading my poetry book, **Song Unsung.**

I would greatly appreciate your reviews on *Amazon* and *Goodreads*. Your reviews are inspiration to me and lessons to become better.

Much love,

China Cancio

China Cancio is a Filipino poet.

She started writing poems and songs in high school.

Her haiku have been published online in publications such as Autumn Moon Haiku Journal, Modern Haiku, Frogpond, Frameless Sky, and The Heron's Nest.